MY FIRST LOOK AT PLANETS

CLOUDS MAKE PRETTY PATTERNS ON EARTH

Earth

TERESA WIMMER

CREATIVE EDUCATION

Published by Creative Education

P.O. Box 227, Mankato, Minnesota 56002

Creative Education is an imprint of The Creative Company

Designed by Rita Marshall

Photographs by Getty Images (Taxi, The Image Bank), Photri (C. Biedel), Tom Stack &

Associates (ESA, Bill & Sally Fletcher, NASA, TSADO)

Copyright © 2008 Creative Education

Printed in the United States of America

Library of Congress Cataloging-in-Publication Data

Wimmer, Teresa, 1975- Earth / by Teresa Wimmer.

p. cm. — (My first look at planets)

Includes index.

ISBN-13: 978-1-58341-516-0

I. Earth—Juvenile literature. I. Title.

QB631.4.W556 2007   525—dc22   2006018707

First edition 9 8 7 6 5 4 3 2 1

EARTH

THE PERFECT SPOT

From space, **planet** Earth looks like a colorful marble. It has white clouds. There are brown lands and lots of blue water. Besides Earth, there are seven other planets. But Earth is special. It is the only planet people live on.

Earth is part of the **solar system**. All of the planets in the solar system move in an **orbit** around the sun. Earth is the third planet from the sun.

STORMS SOMETIMES SWIRL OVER EARTH'S OCEANS

Earth is in the perfect spot. If it were closer to the sun, the water would dry up. If it were farther away, the water would turn to ice.

DIFFERENT DAYS

No two days on Earth are the same. That is because the planet's **weather** is always changing. Some days on Earth have lots of sunshine. Some days are rainy. Some are windy.

One year on Earth lasts 365 days.

It takes that long for Earth

to go around the sun once.

WATER COVERS MUCH OF EARTH'S SURFACE

Different places on Earth have different kinds of weather, too. Some places get lots of snow or rain. Other places are always dry. Some places are always cold. Other places are warm.

Earth is very pretty. It has mountains and deep oceans. Many animals and plants live on Earth. They have fresh air to breathe. They have water to drink.

The coldest land on Earth

is named Antarctica. It is

almost totally covered in ice!

Earth and Its Moon

Earth might seem to be standing still. But it is always moving. Like all the planets, Earth spins like a top. It never stops spinning.

Earth has one moon. The moon is sometimes called "Luna." It moves in an orbit around Earth. The moon looks bright in the night sky. But it is a very dark and lonely place.

The day called Monday used
to be "Moon-day." It was
named after Earth's moon.

EARTH IS MUCH BIGGER THAN ITS MOON

Nothing lives on the moon. The moon has no water or fresh air. There are tall mountains on the moon. There are also big holes called **craters**. The moon is very dusty. Its sky is always black.

YOU CAN SEE EARTH FROM THE MOON'S SURFACE

MORE TO LEARN

People want to learn more about Earth and the moon. About 40 years ago, three men went to the moon. They brought some of the moon's rocks back to Earth to study.

To learn more about Earth, people send special cameras into space. The cameras take pictures of Earth. The pictures show how the clouds on Earth are moving. This can help people tell what the weather will be like.

It takes about four days

for people to get to

the moon in a rocket.

EARTH IS JUST ONE SMALL PART OF THE SOLAR SYSTEM

The cameras take pictures of Earth's seven big pieces of land, or continents (CON-tih-nents), too. The continents move a little bit every year. The pictures show how they have moved. People can guess from the pictures how Earth might look in the future!

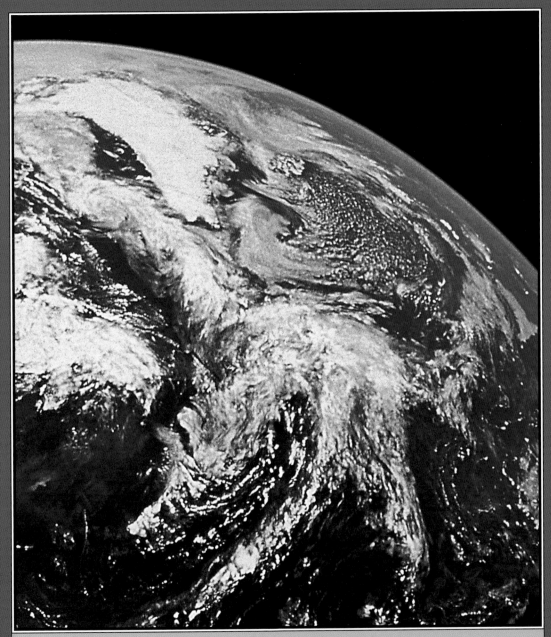

PICTURES FROM SPACE SHOW A LOT ABOUT EARTH

Hands-on: Make a Planet Earth

Earth is a very colorful planet. You can make your very own Earth and watch it spin!

What You Need

A medium Styrofoam ball

A piece of yarn about eight
   inches (20 cm) long

Blue, green, and
   brown markers

Glue

What You Do

1. Color seven big brown and green lands on the Styrofoam ball.
2. Color blue oceans between the lands. Leave white for the clouds, too.
3. Glue one end of the yarn to the top of the ball.
4. Now you have your own planet Earth. Hold on to the top of the yarn. Make Earth spin!

THERE IS NO OTHER PLANET LIKE EARTH

Index

Words to Know

craters—big holes in the ground made when something crashes into a planet

orbit—the path a planet takes around the sun or a moon takes around a planet

planet—a round object that moves around the sun

solar system—the sun, the planets, and their moons

weather—what the air outside is like; weather can be warm, cold, snowy, or rainy

Read More

Rudy, Lisa Jo. *Planets!* New York: HarperCollins, 2005.

Taylor-Butler, Christine. *Earth.* New York: Scholastic, 2005.

Vogt, Gregory. *Solar System.* New York: Scholastic, 2001.

Explore the Web

Enchanted Learning: Earth http://www.zoomschool.com/subjects/astronomy/planets/earth

Funschool: Space http://funschool.kaboose.com/globe-rider/space/index.html?trnstl=1

StarChild: The Planet Earth http://starchild.gsfc.nasa.gov/docs/StarChild/solar_system_level1/earth.html